The Middle Ages

poems by

Jane Chance

Finishing Line Press
Georgetown, Kentucky

The Middle Ages

Publisher: Leah Maines

Editor: Christen Kincaid

Cover Art: Christine de Pizan, "L'epistre d'Othea, la deese," British Library MS
4431, fol. 132v (Hermaphroditis and Salmacis)

Author Photo: Maria Soares Leite, Photographer Sao Paolo Brazil

Cover Design: Elizabeth Maines McCleavy

Printed in the USA on acid-free paper.
Order online: www.finishinglinepress.com
          also available on amazon.com

Author inquiries and mail orders:
Finishing Line Press
P. O. Box 1626
Georgetown, Kentucky 40324
U. S. A.

Table of Contents

III Recovering the Past

IV Middle Age

I

The Real Medieval

Stitches

Stories she sits, spine-bent, to sew,
knotting in each stitch a different life:
the purl she could have lived
if she had been rich.
The knit she should have lived
if she had been religious.
The life she did live,
without fat-legged babies
or the rough must of a man.

Some stitches she uses to cast on,
to marry two rows as one,
needle through slip knot.
Her eyes tire and tear up by day's end,
when needles stop their clack in dark.
Then she bends to kiss
those little fingers,
pricked and bloody.
Those, she calls her own.

Aventure

The knight, newly dubbed, sets out one day,
his armor clattering as he heaves from block
to saddle, his long-maned stallion snorting
and stamping in the first dawn-glimmer.
Does he first map out where might be giants?
And has he smarted and diced flesh at all
with that Toledo steel he wields?

Imagine a Sir Guyon wearying
of his father's complaints:
When will you slay your first dragon?
On his first quest, the heavy responsibility
of fronting the fire-breather.
His squire's service finished, this one morning
the chevalier can forget the smug-faced
older brother who sleeps while waiting
to inherit the castle.

And about that mission to fetch the abducted maiden:
maybe she wasn't a maiden.
Maybe she was a grey-eyed girl he met
one summer as a page at knight camp at Suscinio
and he felt her father might set
the right dowry-price after all.

But surely today what sends him
is simply the scent of meadow and the huffing
of the steed, the heft
of a fine sword against plated thigh,
the sun bursting on the horizon
like a promise
in the long summer of his youth—
all whispering,
Go, see, try.

The Château de Comper

She is protected.
Her drawbridge is double:
one bridge fixed over the moat
and another closer to her,
one that lifts. Her arms are locked
above the gate, gaffs
grand in pose. She doubts
all softness,

all words of entreaty.
She refuses to negotiate terms.
Machicolation keeps her safe,
along with the beauty of distance.
The *chemin de ronde* behind
her battlements shows her proud,
if alone, sentried by the Giant
named I-Will-Never-Forget.

She has in fact been destroyed
several times, her careful stones
borne away by tanned arms.
So you who fancy you might enter,
you with the black hair and sweet face
who boast in metal,
know this: she is Vivienne,
the Château de Comper
bordered by Broceliande.

At moments, behind her dark mirrors,
she weeps quietly so no one hears,
awaiting rescue.
Crenolated. Severe.
A castle imaginary.
A lady who has ceased to exist.

The King of Cape Rinderhorn Speaks to his Dog About Getting Old[1]

to don tinny garbs
fatigue-tough
knight of the everyday
in this house of holey
throwaway, just for you,
my doggy
prince, my four-legged fur beast—
tunnels to get there
(not kingship alone)

I recall occasions of true chivalry
when breasts still mattered
not now, when kingship pairs
with playhouse
just to sit down and shunt
the unused all, this still flesh
like heavy water
the buckle of mortality
(O shameful π!)

age narrativizes—and now for a nap
sleepy toots, naked nooby
best friend
(no one there at all)

The Amazon's Prayer

A frieze on a white marble sarcophagus in the Houston Museum of Art depicts a battle rout of Amazons by Roman soldiers (ca. 140-170 A.D.).

The helmeted guard binds her bleeding hands to heels,
muttering, *Lazyges, you and your kin finally broke the treaty.*
You'll die for it, but first, suffer far worse. Head down.
Bow to the legate as he passes, one-breasted monster.[2]
Such a man! one you, with javelin and your bow, can never equal,
whatever your skill. He jerks the leather tighter.

On this side of the Danube, the Sarmatians of the Quadi and Marcomanni
are the only trophy prisoners of the Second Roman legion at Laugaricio,
beneath the old stone rotunda atop the hill. In this winter rain
the Amazon dreams of Carpathian slopes, their wagons near the great fires
kept burning, heroic tales inspiring us to valor. She seems to see
great warriors of old, the Scythian founders Marpasia and Lampheto,

the daughters of Ares. And Thamaris—she who ambushed Persian Cyrus
and made him kneel (as she does now, in shame) before cutting off his head
in a basin of his own men's blood. Amazons Menalippe and Hippolyte,
whose lances and shields unhorsed Hercules and Theseus.
O Artemis Astarte (she prays), goddess of the hunt and the white moon,
sign to the world how Rome cut us down, our fast horses trampling our own dead.

Show how we brave women fought to the end.
Shape us in fine white marble, small figures
to guard each corner of the legate's sarcophagus.
Keep our story from wisping away like smoke from fire.
Remember us—not Roman trophies,
　　　　bound and bent in tribute—but Amazons,

as if dancing—

　　　dancing,

on this grave of a son-of-a-bitch. [3]

Unicorn

The unicorn in the tapestry[4]
encircled by a burnished fence
smiles despite the chain on his neck.
Bound tight to the tree
his tail curls into bouquets,
his image framed by a winding trellis
of green leaves and golden flowers.
From heaven white blossoms plummet
daisies, lilies, Queen Ann's lace.

The tree that tethers him has fruitfully multiplied:
ruby pomegranates cradled by leafy boughs.
The letters A and E married
at the end of the braid that girdles
the slim middle of its trunk.
He no longer awaits a virgin
into whose lap he must lay his head
to be captured. His mission fulfilled,
he is of course happy.

For Anne was surely a beautiful virgin,
her husband, Charles of France, likely a rich king.
They, too, will be fruitful and multiply.
Her unicorn attests to her eternal
perfection and purity,
sign and symbol of success.
But what is the unicorn thinking, do you suppose?
He is looking up, his horn very stiff,
his little eye turned to Anne's boudoir ceiling.

Plain tuckered out from this fantasy,
just wanting oats and alfalfa cubes,
as if he were not imaginary and tired of being
symbolic.
He'd like to sleep a little, or play with the others,
leave town and get a little dirty,
have a cool drink, find a girl,
let down his horn now and then.

Riddle #1

Take me
My fish shape
Plunge into my clutch
Your leather mama
Half twin fraternal
Tongue and laces
Marry my journey
I carry the day
(What am I?)[5]

To Scheherazade from the Bride Before

Line your eyes with black kohl and redden your lips.
Adorn your body with thin, slippery silks,
Then whisper softly your low sensual O's.
Smile so you open your lips to your tongue.
Twirl the tip up in touching your lip.

Embrace him first like your tall older brother.
Praise his oiled shoulders, his robe of fine linen.
Ply him with ripe figs and sweet honey wine.
Let him lean close in, like perfume on skin,
Then leave a breath's space to stoke his desire.

When taken to couch, kiss his every inch.
But avoid, please, the main parts, delay if you can.
Tell him your story, but stop many times.
Stroke him, massage him, his neck and his back,
his ears and his eyelids. The inside of elbows.

Let bodies barely touch but let them touch barely.
And consider these questions unanswered I pose:
Which pleases more? The ending of story, or story unending?
Is it better the touching, or the end of all touching?
Are your words what he longs for, or the promise of more?

I leave you these questions, written so quickly,
The bride before you, awaiting Shahryar.
From the bride before me, I learned all these lessons.
If you are now reading, you know I guessed wrongly.
A virgin knows nothing until she is not.

Aubade[6]

Marooned. With secret color
I seek your scarab arms,
Unstructured pitch desiring

A cutting, measure of melody.
Such melismatic loving in our song:
Saturdays tuned over green months,

Polyphonic memories of mannered
Rooms. Cryptic lover, let me
Note you clearly; open windows,

Spread spring. Do not leave me
Like this—marooned, mensural,
Singing with a shiver

Of your white roach body.

At the Breton Abbey of St. Gildas de Rhuys

> —"The country was wild and the language unknown to me, the natives were brutal and barbarous, the monks were beyond control and led a dissolute life which was well known to all."
> —Peter Abelard, *Historia calamitatum* (History of My Calamities)

Across from the abbey church, sipping coffee,
I spot a laughing woman buying bread.
Her waist-long blond hair furls in the sea-breeze,
her blouse ruffled, green, with red roses,
her peasant skirt fringed in lavender.
Shaking her bracelets as she shifts
her sandaled feet she reaches over
to touch the baker's hand.

I wish I had been her, not always hunched
over books. Like Abelard, master of *Yes and No*,
sought out by students of so many tongues,
who locked his with that of his host's niece.
Shorn of a future—their son, Astrolabe, aside—
an abbot in exile at the abbey, soon poisoned.
I think: monkish *Schadenfreude*.
The old abbey church sits in stone silence.

I imagine her husband at home
in bed cuddling his empty bottle
of Côtes du Rhone. Likely her children
are brutal and say they don't love her,
this moment the bright purchase of her day.
For a second she turns toward me:
her lined face as worn as fine leather
left to rain, and the baker, the man
she loved as a girl.

Like Abelard fleeing to Paris
to live greater lies, I rise,
shedding books as I go,
the cold ochre stones of the church

a text for the blind.
No longer a lesson in humility
but in masking.

Still, she wears her joy as costume,
her regrets, as jewelry.

The Night the Books Fell

The night the shelves shuddered off the wall
after twenty-three years of bolstering books,
when books hurtled down from their designated places
in a noise not unlike that of the end of the world,
from a book's point of view, as indeed it was;
when the dowels and brackets gave way,
in that moment when the old historical house
shook and trembled, cracked by thunderstorms
in the middle of dreams, it must have thought
(if thought it could have), *At last!*

The books hailing down in an astonishing
blast of sheetrock dust reached as far
as the front door, the floor rushing
up to meet them, their spines cracked,
Sir Gawain's back entirely broken, and the Hobbit's;
Virgil's and Dante's covers torn and ripped,
and the others, piling one atop another, lost in the
tumult, as if they, too, just wore out.

Why this one brief storm, after Carla, Alison,
and Ike? The tough edge of discipline
slackened, next to the need to give way.
A nervous breakdown of knowledge
gone astray. Atlas weary of lifting up
the sky from the earth,
just to keep his strength, but then
that sheer rush of relief at letting go and
it doesn't matter anymore,
as if dropping off the edge of the world.

Somewhere else far away, on the rocky coast
of Brittany, the professor whose books they were
awoke with a start, and then, remembering where
she was, felt glad once more to be retired
after years and years, not yet knowing
about the fall of the books, as if,

by means of this cosmic sign
relieved of the obligation
of learnedness
and granted the divine gift of
pleasure in being
simply human.

Homage to Neptune

Gray, the sea porting waves that mute
the day, its color scotched. I veer along the high
seawall, lost in thought, remembering

those lost from long ago. And where *has* all
the blue sky gone? Chased to the Aegean,
in books, where life skits across Ulysses's

wine-dark sea, or to the East, to frame
white sand beached by palms.
This February sea-frieze, portending

something bruited up from below, my god
of illusions, Neptune rising in this morning mist,
his waves parting for passage of a divine tomorrow,

say, along with the ascent of sweet dreams
from Morpheus's cave (where I'll be hiding, drunk
from cups of forgetfulness and bliss-drowse). Imagine

the billows of bed, the balm of a warmed back,
and those left us by the gods as gifts, in trust without guile,
snuggling against us with cold noses and little canine feet.

Truth

"And trouthe thee shal delivere."
—Geoffrey Chaucer, "Balade de Bon Conseyl" ("Truth")

By the stream of Kidron Jesus and his disciples entered a garden.
There Judas betrayed him and Simon Peter three times denied him.
He asked, *Shall I not drink the cup that my Father has given me?*

Pilate asked the Jews for their accusation against him.
Why not try him by your own laws? Jesus said, knowing their laws
did not apply, *My kingdom is not earthly.*

And when Pilate asked, "What is truth?" Jesus replied,
My voice is of the truth. Chosen instead of murderer Barabbas,
he was flogged and given thorn crown, purple robe, a slap across the face.

Pilate said, *I see no guilt; you crucify him. He is the Son of God, he says.*
Refusing to write what they claimed he had said he was—"King of the Jews"—
Pilate ended with *I have written what I have written.*

The soldiers, after divvying up his clothes, hung him on the cross.
They bet on his seamless tunic. At the foot of the cross stood mother Mary,
her sister Mary, Mary Magdalene, and John, to whom Jesus said,

Behold, this is your Mother, though she was not. To her, he said, *Woman,
behold, this is your son,* though he was not. Then he died. In anguish,
the earth trembled. The sun in grief covered itself. Graves opened, bones split.

Joseph, disciple from Arimathea, secretly asked Pilate's permission
to take down his corpse. Nicodemus bound him in linen with fine spices
and laid him in a fresh tomb in the garden. So the night of grief ended.

What is truth? At dawn, the sun rose. Some say the earth turned.

Migration

Cloven hooves of an ox, back legs of a horse,
mane of a lion, face of a warthog.
The wildebeest, Kenyans say, *so ugly only a mother could love him,*
moves in dark herds across the Mara like a wave,

heading south to the Serengeti and back again to Kenya.
The sun filtering through his golden mane
as he lopes along in his uneven way,
it all suddenly seems just right, a different kind of balance,

like light through stained glass in a chill Gothic cathedral
that draws you in – the surprise, once past the massive carved doors
into darkness, only then seeing you're not alone,
but one of many, you and the wildebeests

in endless repetition, season in and season out,
natural music in time, in time.

II

Romancing the Rose

The Morning After

The deed is done, read the will: in the quiet
Grotto garden, cracks sunder the dial
Behind the knight's house, cockle-bricked
And tudor-masoned. The deed is done: she bit
The anemone in brisk cycles when the boar bored
The time away to flowers. He lipped the cup
And shrank the spider. Read the will: the girl
Rose, petals crushed to dust, re-fused
The house in copper assent. Her hair drenched
In rain she hung upon the dial to dry.
And the dread garden she circled into compact touch
To create her naked face. He curled into the cup
To hide, until the tin dawn drummed
The knight away, and she breast-fed the sun.

Meme

got the message virtual,
bedbug, itch electronic
and whiz!
the moon opens tonight
like a vast door to star binaries of the web
so let me share this with you
or did I mean
a three-way
(some cotton-candy polish for a big date)
and after, key iteration, click click click
like it? just lick here
no stamp required, if you pass it around,
viz., magic marker on a bathroom door
the meme's promiscuous
(suck on this thought and then we're through)
Oh, snap! my computer is dense
with fraught cries of "help me," "do me."
All we need is facebook, instagram,
and porn,
until someday, violets
on azure lace,
la la la la.

So kiss whenever, eternally yours,
"with love"

You, Stranger

This elbow crooked in the dark
this position, this tongue
doing *this*, and *this*,
and kissing me in excruciatingly
sensitive places
only I've known before.
Behind this stranger's face
is Bobby's grin,
and Sammy, whom I loved best of all
before Mack.
These men so different
and so strange
know me so well, like you, in bed.
It is this arch, this nuzzle, this fantasy
that reminds me of them.
In sleeping with
you, stranger,
I sleep with all men.

Shuck

The man leans over the full basin
unleashes another supple oyster
from its shell, a special knife he tucks
for shucking, curved so
to cut free, minute-quick,
the tendons in his arms tightening
as he thinks about Marguerite—
the woman he met last night at the "Volcano,"
and how soft, oysterlike,
when he slid her out of her silken shell
the salt of her, naked,
shucked like his oyster.
How he always finds ocean and salt,
is home. Not a thinker,
he, in jeans and a wifebeater,
that memory and the lush oyster fusing, raw,
himself the oyster knife:
hard, shiny, strong.
Like a god. Immortal.

Gravel

The child of gravel is grit.
It begins there, tiny babe,
on driveways to anchor transport,
whether shoes or tires.
To what end?
Of what am I thinking?

Ah, the aching clitoris.
All female mammals have one.
(Did you know? Some fish, too.)
I am stunned. All this rutting
not from males rampant with desire
but summoned, by a female
who waits for that tickle.
I have forgotten now. What was I thinking?

Oh yes, gravel. The road to finitude.
The polite coverup of dirt and muck.
One point connected to another.
Does a sheep need three covers to make a babe?
Think of Yorkish Swaledales.
White ringed eyes, black faces,
females horned like males.

Simba

The lion with the bloody eye
the slack mouth that windows
blunt and broken teeth
sits and waits behind the bush
for the readiness of his newly-won mate.

Only when she walks yards away
and bellies down
can he top her, bite her neck,
rigor his snarl aloud, and ugly,
his wrinkled snout, like death on the way.

In three seconds, lifting off
with care for penis barbs,
she rolls over on her back
to rave those paws soft above and
spoon him close nearby.

Two weeks: every fifteen minutes,
love, love, love.
Lion honeymoon, the guide says.

Enchanted Rock[7]

This lazy mountain
long and pink as a lady's thighs
a lady lying on her side, listening
for her lover.
Trees blanket her long afternoon.
Sleep and dream, woman
whose desire time mounted
in granite.
You mistress

without sin.
Atop you a muscled wind brandishes
cloudy fists
to beat you around,
stoned sister
too tough to notice,
and anyone who tries to move you.
Mean the wind you never mind
and mute the man who climbs you.

Cactus Wren

In love, we're like the cactus wren—
free as the windy Chihuahuan
bright as a good idea
quick as the finish of spring.

The cactus wren hunts for a bare forked tree
for her fast bright hover,
then nests in a spiny bed
to barb the cottonwood snake's slither.

She knows without spikes and thorns
her hatch won't learn fear,
innocence prickling into calamity.
Soft needs hard, weak needs mean.

Unlike her, we quiet for the snake's hiss.
We cut barbs to freedom, calm
the flap of the wing, urge
the sun's rising—

that slow, slow gentle dawn.

Elegy for Lost Light

Our dream bodies. Late, running,
forgot the tree
like a song, ours.

Dance the windowpane, you said.

Tell me, possessed by light,
if light ever…

Tell me,
if running—

I was late, how the tree…
how the light…

came through
the windowpane.

Did, once.

Imagine the moon, then.

Console
me.

Going Down Backwards

I lumber over the schooner side
where a pony-tailed sailor offers two heads,
complex pumps, the galley
with the wood-burning stove
always lit by four a.m., and the stairs
to my shelter-sized bunk,
a sign above advising
"Go down backwards."

The schooner sails unfurled,
the captain at the helm
his hand stout on the wheel
knifes through the black waters
of Penobscot Bay, past warning lighthouses,
islands you can't quite see for firs.
We are calm, ourselves. At peace.
The brilliant sun setting, a cup of coffee in hand.

What else is there
to fear?
Other schooners, a loon
or two, the rocks slippery with seaweed
near Hell's Half Acre.
The handmade dinghy named
"Babe."
The name he called me.

At night, waking blind, I hit my head
on the old beam above the pillow,
unseeing without glasses,
how to find up, the single light
on deck. Stuck among books on the bed
I touch the door-handle, hold fast
to each wooden step, rise, pajama-clad,
to the empty deck at three,
fearing someone will awaken—
the gruff sound, its whuff-whuff, then water.

I turn homeward.

What if there were
wine, sung
songs? If the deck
were slashed with rain,
wind cracking all, side to side?

Oh, a swerving, a car,
head crocked
against the roof, turning
wheel lunged through
the chest, knees
dashed.
Someone I loved.

But I trust the sign.
Going down
I hit my head on the beam
above my bunk again
and fall asleep,
drowning, drowning,
in night.

Silent Sister

Fool that I am, I said
Do you have a sister?

Not to speak of, you said.
Then I shall be your silent sister.

Your unspeakable sister.
The one you had sex with

and then ignored.
The role I'm left with

since you're spoken for.
(As if I'd asked you to dance.)

Rattle

The baby brandishes his rattle
like victory. The car rattles, too,
then shakes as I ease
fifth gear down into reverse,
tricky British car.
The rattle gives it away:
something loose, or broken,
shaking like an old man with palsy,
jerking backward, hits the tree.

Death rattles,
something lost or broken inside.
I rattle into your arms,
glad to see you,
French words rattling off my tongue
like rain spattering a lake.
The love of your life—not me—I only learn about
after her husband calls.
That rattle.

Into the Dark

Earth extinguishes your life
prematurely, your body scuffed to bone.

Cold incoming, only weeds left
on blasted ground.

The sun disintegrates,
realities burn up my bed.

I sleep without a moon, just
the dark, brute truth itself.

Hate shut out, heaviness departed.
Early morning, eyes open.

I never really loved you.

I will always love you.

Dirt

My error lay in being gentle.
The stars that hover over orchards
offer no room to Ruthless.
(Oh, weak soul, why you?
I lack the wag's truth.)
Taffy speech to be sweet,
bait for capture, all girls agree.
Let me come clean.
Accommodate me.
The view is wide from the top of the hill.
The last hill, I climbed for you.

Going down, the steps narrow.
No house left for the lost.
These stones once were mountains,
dinned to dirt by storm and fire.
Mineral essence of hill and height
I hold now in my palm:
world recreated in such tiny wonder.
Ready now to leave you
for seed of hill and sky
and, by dint of going,
live within its joy.

Black Is the Color

As if a blackberry could shoot up.
An odor like must,
or should.
My New York glam coat that I never wear.
Of night, darkening for sin, lost
plums dropping one by one to ground.
This error of distance.
Or marvel in great disorder.
When he said, *You break a home, you fill it with bad luck,*
he really meant
with black.
Only in old Appalachian songs

is black the color of

Spit

What she always wanted was to spit out,
blind to the mandate of the stiff penis.

Once, she hitched south away from snow,
the man in the truck saying, "No, don't!"

So, she holds her breath and swallows,
thinking; her mind turned swamp.

She whittles herself small, joy scant,
to please him, thin coat to weather

desire. Her own, a chipped cup
left behind on the shelf.

Now, *Oh* and *No*
are different routes to the same town,
and she drives her own car everywhere.

In the Subjunctive Mode

After Louise Gluck

what if I were to live tented
in a burkha of black
borrowed from some Saudi friend?
if no one were ever meant to enter,
my eyes alone sending signals:

NO ADMITTANCE
NO TRESPASSING?

imagine: the brilliance of fast lights
a Humvee incoming
crashing, like all the others
outside my window
through which I can barely see.

then, hurt feet drug up the stairs one by one
and some chainsaw monster I cannot face
covered as I am except for latticed eyes
and darkness falling in shreds around me
like a rent veil

though my mouth is closed
my mouth is closed, I said
if I were to speak only with my eyes, then I might say

Why don't you come up and see me, sometime (if I were Mae West)
Closed for repairs (if I were a failed restaurant)
Only the lonely (if I were Roy Orbison)
We have no Peruvian potatoes today (if I were a gourmet delivery man)

in any case, I would bat my eyes with varying degrees
of desire alarm empathy embarrassment

what I would say, if necessary
(but in a foreign language, preferably Italian):

Non voglio niente (I desire nothing)
Non ti voglio (I do not want you)
Per favore, vai via! (Please, go away!)

what I would be thinking:
sometimes I scare even myself

Exquisite Corpse

Z Krewe, Aquarius, Babalu, too—
time for a blaze-orange disco wig,
my alter self, layers piled on
like blonde Italian butter cake,
Gambrinus, Grand Momus—
am I doing this once more?
Gotcha, lass of my youth,
raw, eager, untouched,
and those old stories glow.

My dog still knows me
in my glitter glam,
fever-red, my lips, eyes like black spiders,
his eyes follow me across the room—
I am his anchor, his Be There Always.
So, welcome to this Jane—jane—this John—
I wear beads, and more beads—
       wanna dance?

Strip Orange

My love gives me an orange
I roll around my breasts in joy.
My torso begins to smell like fun.
I peel off one skin after another
to see, deep down, his heart
and two doves cooing L O V E.
When I buss them, they all
puff off in a mad natter.

The strip orange says in a dark voice,
You uncovered my layers.
Time now to plant my seed.
"O sorry, O," I sing,
no seed in mind or mouth for me.
Boat-shaped fruit, lyric
on my tongue, I sail past
orange and peel.

Whattup,
pomegranate?

In Guadeloupe

come back at seven,
pizza and cougars then,
the bartender says,
as if I need to run back, shower,
shave my legs and everything else
just to have a pizza
or a man

but now I think on it
a really sweet idea
who would know
in this French port marina
on the night of Bastille Day
where no one knows me
or speaks English

have another mojito
and mull it over
says the bald French bartender
who according to him makes the best
mojitos in town
(and, apparently, cougars)

III

Recovering the Past

Nothing Has a Single Beginning

Nothing has a single beginning:
a murder, a love affair, a book.

After a life: some blood, an absence, a forgetting.
Before, raw heat, fingers on a thigh, a swelter of idea.

Just as noise is not noise but a chaos
of distinct voices without proximity.

Dark Matters[8]

(For Vera Rubin, 1928-2016)

Fascinated by night, Vera Rubin
loved watching stars.
But a woman can't study astronomy, they said.
So Vera watched stars at Vassar and Cornell,
where her advisor called her thesis *sloppy*.

Besides, she was pregnant
and shouldn't deliver her paper
before the American Astronomical Society.
Instead, her advisor suggested he would present it
under his own name, keeping hers safely hidden.

But then she said, "I *can* go," and she did.
When turned down for admission to grad school—
Princeton does not accept women—
she watched the stars at George Washington University,
and, at Carnegie Institute, with Kenneth Ford.

The first woman to use the telescope at Palomar,
she created her own women's bathroom there
by taping a woman's image on a men's bathroom door.
She argued that dark matter existing in space was created by
the Big Bang, unseen because it emits no light,

yet pulling other bodies through gravity.
Proof used now by astronomers to explain
how distant galaxies move at the same speed as those close.
Awarded a Nobel Prize in 2017. But not to Rubin.
Another dark matter.

Ferroglyph: Jim Love's "Area Code"[9]

full moon:
wild boar screams

for Texas
I turn back

oil pump-jack,
for head above water

birdhouse empty
in drought, umbrella for rain

a raised cottage and I
have a history

America, your stars barb
wire my heart

the gate to my locked bed.
O, violence of Skilsaw

I lie
chevroned into pipe

my parents' comfort
a shovel to leak tears

repair tool for flats
I drink up, to bleed

pine tree outside
my only green

pump-jack to speak of
longhorns stare

my little family tubs

some fun some toys some art

water, the old pump spigots.
lark bunting trills in the desert

I will be known
my small family springing up on stems,

like flowers

like flowers

Isola

Born on a cold day in October
far, far, from everyone
she was drawn to the scent of ginger
and sandalwood. Her mother made her

a flamingo pink dress with Spanish sleeves
to play in the streets. Her father never forgave her
when she grew too large for lace.
She's now big as a gabled house.

Sad, their final trip across galaxies
to the tight room where dinner is set
at six for white-haired women only.
What pleasures remain: the toys they left,

her father's egg-yellow aggies, the sheen
of mahogany in her mother's hope chest.
When the next flood begins its campaign,
she will float away in one, embracing the other,

headed home at last, to the island
of *cuore solo.*

I Go Back To October 1944

I want to say to you, in your beaded crêpe de chine,
Get your passport first.
The one you haven't received because you didn't apply
in time. Can you even cross the border
without one? And what is a honeymoon
without a bride? So cancel the wedding.
But marry him, eventually. And please,
get a good physical, just in case.

So he goes alone on the honeymoon
rather than lose his deposit. What do you do
while he's away? Do you moon over him
in front of his photo and wonder if he loves you?
Understand, you both are young—and poor.
He even had to eat lard sandwiches
during the Depression. Otherwise,
no folly at all about marrying.

Wait. Now I think about it, he doesn't go alone.
No, he cancels the trip, gets his deposit back,
and you both go to Niagara Falls,
on the Canadian side. Yes, this makes more sense.
The other is likely false, a tale your sister
tells me decades later, after you have died,
when she is angry at him for playing golf
instead of fixing her furnace.

So, never mind! Go ahead,
cut the cake, laugh, kiss, dance.
In three months you'll be pregnant
and give birth—not to that silly boy
my father will decide to name after himself—
but to that baby girl with golden curls
you always wanted.

When I Was Young and Still Had Hair

I was good looking when I was twenty.
On Saturday nights I'd wear a suit
and take my weekly earnings from the factory
to the dance at the Elks Club.
Oh I could dance! And the girls loved that!
Saved up money for an old Ford.
Swung them around to the Lindy Hop
and up close and tight for the Fox Trot.
Big bands, Benny Goodman, Tommy Dorsey.
I was a big man in my little town.

But growing up, it was every day, church with Mom at the Friends.
Walking to school two miles away, had to.
Thelma and I were the youngest of the five who lived.
Mom would stretch the bacon—
keep the grease in a jar on the stove.
Garden in the back for vegetables.
Bean with bacon soup and spam.
Dad worked at the tin factory till he got laid off—
that finger he caught in the slicer one time.
Mom sewed patches on pants to make them last.

I wanted to go to college but not enough dough.
Thelma got a job at the factory. Doris got
pregnant and married Tom the mechanic.
But I loved the ladies. Oh I could dance!
Finally signed up for the Army—
had to get out of Elwood.
Join the Army and see the world.
See the World! Think of it!
Travel to Guam and Australia, meet the ladies.
Swung them around to the Lindy Hop.

When I still had hair,
I was good looking.

Tickle Monster

When I am six, my father reads to us
tales of crooked witches
and knights who skewer
long-toothed dragons
that rip off heads and skin,

stubbled intimacy
built on sticks,
a tilted house on chicken legs
to cluck away a million miles,
our brass-buckled dad

tickle-monster
who wrassles us
to laughter, till, still too rough,
he makes us cry, little brother and I,
and kisses away our tears

something soft in our dad
shapes the magic he crafts—
a gift to tender the heart
our mother asleep in the dark
with a killer headache.

Markers

in the Philippines I tie a string around a black coconut beetle
as my ahma taught me, his pincers big enough
to crunch my finger, and fly it around the house to scare

Mommy, curling up the red patent-leather belt
after she whips us for fighting, my brother and me

later, in Georgia, on the red dirt road in front of our new house
the man in his truck sings out "peaches and green beans"
we sleep on new mattresses on the floor

but Mommy, burning the potatoes again,
lies down because her head hurts.

I touch her shoulder and call her name
the morning she won't wake up
I phone Daddy at work all by myself

the hospital where she sleeps, her head shaved on one side,
and driving back with Daddy in the dark
the tiny light of her window farther and farther away

Grandma comes to visit, giving me a new doll-outfit every day

the black telephone rings
Daddy cries, calls to me, his arms open
but I stand so still, I do not cry I do not move
my brother runs to him

Mommy, beautiful in the blue brocade dress,
in a box lowered into the earth, and why?
if she is really just sleeping

I dress my little brother in girl's clothes and a bonnet
pat berry mud-pies for Daddy after work

I catch big green grasshoppers with yellow and black stripes

on their bellies that ooze yellow like eggs when you step on them
so I can light a match and see what happens
when they burn in a jar

Daddy walks with me after dinner to smoke a cigar
in the dark he says *I miss your mother so much*
I see her everywhere I turn

we drive to pick out a granite marker, one with a lamb image,
before we move to New Jersey

years later, we stop on the way back from Disney World,
my daughter and the boys
finding the lot number at last
but then
I cry and cry
for there is
                    nothing there
nothing at all but grass

Tomboy

At eight I long for a horse
with a velvet nose and bright eyes.

My father gives me a box camera.
A portable stable. Joy!

In Tien-mou I trade my dad's Luckys
for an hour astride a Mongolian pony
fast and lean as a thought.

I race him past rice paddies
and the farmer and his water buffalo
slowly furrowing the mud with a wooden plow. Hello!

My father has more Lucky Strikes in his sock drawer:
strike, the flare of the match to light the cigarette
and burn the smoke my father loves.

If you don't let the boys win, they won't like you.

True pony!
I grab your mane and grip the pommel
tight, my legs astraddle the world, and urge you on,

leaving behind the furniture
of gender.

Perfect

When I was twelve, a cat crept
in and had four kittens in our basement—
furry pillows, like earmuffs
to hold close to your heart
so you wouldn't hear ugly things.
Every day after school I checked to see if they were o.k.—
the mother cat so patient, let them bite her,
and licked them when they peed.
I told my parents the good news
and our stepmother said, *When our barn cat gave birth,*
we drowned the kittens in the toilet
(just more cats to breed).
We don't really need any right now.

I thought I would kill myself.
I poured mercurochrome into a glass
but it tasted terrible and I didn't die.
I looked up "veterinary" in the phone book
and wrote them a letter asking for help.
He came soon to pick them up.
My parents didn't get mad—
I thought I might get spanked.
They said I could keep one, but only outdoors.
When I came home from school one day
my stepmother and stepsister had moved out,
took their stuff and the dining-room table.

A few months later she wrote me to come visit, so
I went on the bus all by myself.
She wanted me to ask my father to let them come back.
She gave me coins from her tips each night.
But Dad said no and soon we had a new stepmother.
When we got transferred to Germany
we left my cat behind—
Dad said someone will feed him.
He reminded us about *duty*
and following the rules—you know, his job.

I had to leave my friends on our street, too,
wrote them once or twice
(can always make new ones).

Finally got a dachshund with long red hair and ears.
Loved that dog, Moxie was his name.
Dad wrote me at college he had let Moxie out one night
and a car hit him in the dark.
You know, Dad said, *funny thing—not a mark on him.*
He was perfect. Just perfect.
I cried.

My boyfriend took me to the Sweet Shop
for a cherry Coke.

Homecoming

The last time the colonel hit her,
she was sixteen. It was about the dishes
her brother should have washed
but didn't. They were sitting at the dinner table
on a Sunday, just finishing chicken and mashed potatoes,
green beans. Their father didn't care whose turn
it was. He just wanted them washed, and *now*.
He glared at her, like a gun barrel lowering.
And when she said *No, it's not my turn, I won't,*

he yelled, his eyes jittering into anger
that felt like shattering glass.
The rush of mountains closing in, a sense
of thunder. A force she dared resist so stupidly
that, when he hit her, she was still saying no,
and so, surprised. But he kept hitting,
took his belt off and walloped her
into a wailing so loud that, no longer caring,
she knew the neighbors heard.

Years later, flying back to the home never her home
after her father's stroke, and holding his hand
when he awoke from the coma and begged,
first, for his dog, and then, *please*, just take him home,
with her brother and sister-in-law fanning his face,
wiping away the sweat, at the end of his life
finally forgiving him his mortality, his failures:
the last words he spoke to them, the colonel,
their father, as he gazed up at them, hovering
around the narrow hospital bed, were

I have such good kids.

These words that passed for love.

Walking and Talking with Grandma

Grandma worships with the Friends today
wearing her big sun bonnet and her long buttoned up dress
"Got to hurry, got to hurry," she mutters
"Cooked the green beans with bacon, too," again to herself
holds the Bible close to her tightly-bodiced

bosom next to her purse
"Hey Granny! Give me your purse!"
The dirty boy yells at her, grabbing at it.
"Give it now! Fucking bitch! Crazy old lady!"
"God will forgive you, my son," Grandma says,
bashing him on his head with her purse.
And whirling around she kicks him
with her old fashioned lace-up shoe right in the groin
"Ouch! My head! Ouch!" He screams.
"Little pussy," she whispers.

IV

Middle Age

Litany to Our Lady of Headlines

muzzle wired shut
dog tossed off a truck
puppy hanged from a fence
burned by boys
young stag in a park
teens behead for sport
New Delhi girl on a night bus
raped with an iron rod
gay man barb-wired
to a fence in the snow

in New England villages
church bells knell regret
in big cities EMS vans
shrill us over
to other freeway lanes
help on the way

how soon   how fast

for souls armed with hearts
like knives
against the soft-eyed shy
some love requires hurt
this is what they know
this is what they were given

pray for   mercy to
        listen

"Ego te absolvo a peccatis tuis"

Do you want me to sign your book? the poet asks.
You have already signed it, I say.
What do you want, then?
I want to comfort the child in you, I say.
Your poems are like a knife in my heart.
Then don't read my book! he cries.

What do you want from me? I ask.
I want to return what I suffered and lost, he says.
Grim words, revenge behind them.
Forgive your father, forgive your mother.
These are only words, I say.
As he bows his head,

Just like a poet I sign above him
Ego te absolvo a peccatis tuis.[10]

Shotgun (1866)

I'm a little row house
Thirty feet long
and ten feet wide
Here is my single bay
Who is it lives inside?

The smell of callaloo
Dasheen bush, stem and leaf
Garlic glory, too
Pimento seed, coco milk—
Onion, hot pepper, just a little in the stew

The porch for sunset and Sunday after church
Fried chicken, cob corn,
sweet potato pie
Chat with neighbors, friends
and family

Till you die
Three rooms, no doors
See clear through till end—
Only one exit here.
All seems mighty fine

Never mind the man, now,
Him with the gun
Grass will always grow
Around the house
Wherever sun will shine

The Leopard in the Sausage Tree

His belly swollen big as pregnancy
his legs straddling the branch
like a lover he licks
the bones and gristle of his topi kill
We wait, breath bated, below, in Land Cruisers
we grip our Canons
with long expensive lenses
for that perfect *perfect* shot.

The heavy shells of the sausage tree
blossom beige fruit, good for Maasai beer
for measles and abortions, too,
the guide tells us, while we gaze above, rapt.
A healing tree that hides him
whose green eyes glare out
empty of any meaning, any hope of
feeling in his moment of perfect fullness

save the taste of a long red shank bone
stinking of the blood of the gone beast,
only hours before, gliding through the old Eden
of the Tarangire, a *topi* caught in a moment
of grace, motion en route to essence,
final deconstruction.
To structure without identity,
the personal torn from flesh,

now strictly anonymous,
the kill could be anything,
even you or me. We all agree,
whirring, clicking our cameras.
That perfection,
the leopard above.
Us safe, below.

Ears

Human-eared elephants throned on gold staffs.
Linguists twist the alien words they hear
from the stiff-tongued into those known soft
words in Akan, just for their chief.[11]

Akyeame, do you sleep? The chief cries, *Advisors,*
be swift! Which enemy comes in the night?
Bring words to me. In you
I keep the ears of the elephant.

Ears cover me all over, like the shafts of Akan staffs.
I ache after walking the coffee shops
because I am, as you know, all ears.
Poems run in my blood, pissing out the ugly.

I will make foreign words my own—*edor-brice*,
Anglo-Saxon for fence-breaking, *invogliàre*, Italian,
creating desire in others, with *potentas*, Latin,
for power, and maybe tossing in some Old French for ornament.

Jericho hears couples' chat in Starbucks
and crafts a publish-worthy poem on his phone.
O couples of Starbucks, gift me strange words.
The *New Yorker*, I'm sure, is waiting for me.

Last Resort

Here, you get to know the sea
and its whims: when the wind's sigh
mounts to howl
and water boulevards down trolley tracks,
a nervous lizard flicking its tongue

when shutters slap against a cypress house
like useless limbs against a trunk
and storm-catchers jetty into bars,
chug tequila shots and suck limes
awaiting the quiet calm

of the Eye above
when all noise stops
except the surf mincing into town
mewling like a cat on splashy feet

The blue-eyed guy at the bar looks around
and says, *I guess we're all hooked
on finality.*

Meaning, exorcizing beauty
while living on the edge—
say, hurtling out of a cracked-up house
on flattened Bolivar into black surge.

The professor lifts her glass in a toast.
Maybe so, she smiles back,
although she knows

that waves will always rise
(uncrossing her legs
on the barstool)
just before
they lower
their resistance.

Grand Momus Parade

Mardi Gras is hard-partying all day long,
mimosas and bloody marys,
brunchy eggs,
jambayala and frito pie,
mostly, being sociable,
Hi, Jim, hi, Lizette.

Let's face it: the drums are
pounding in the night,
dim to see, the crowd crushed together
on Twenty-fifth Street
bright in green and golden and purple beads,
float-treasure to make rich with.

Me, I'd catch so many beads
the people'd see,
yes, she is rich, really rich,
full of big brassy
words, alphabets
poking out of ears
and eyes,
poem girl,
she is magic, a mummer
in her shimmer,
as if to say:

flying, I am
free, whee!
tap-dancing down the street,
full of glee, full of
"look at me"
full to the top
in Galveston
with "Grand"
and glad to be
my own Mardi Gras
Momus
on parade.

My Western

My Western state
might be Texas
or maybe California,

but does state matter?
Somewhere not far from Mexico
and the Rio Grande.

Film some rough and cowboy,
film some fantasy,
don't grow up too soon.

In rocky hills
sandstone troubles me:
too pink, so soft.

State borders fall away,
my boots out the door.
Hands off the horse's body!

Hearing the wind in rush
like a prayer
far from *because* and *if.*

Warm brown leather of my saddle
doubles for Trigger's,
following Gene and Roy.

Childhood ends so.
Dear horse, your body and mine:
one nation, indivisible.

Ride on, cowgirl.

In the Poetry Workshop

My friend, you just gave birth to your own mother.
She, undoing babies-to-be at night on her kitchen table
for unwed teens and mothers with three too many.
You write a poem from her point of view instead of your own,
this monster you say you hate
because she never loved you.

You create your own personal Frankenstein
whom we love, despite her oddly
rectangular head, the stitches
above her eyes like mad crows,
her words so guttural
they sound like rocks in her throat.

But just as you finish sewing her up
from that angry corpse of your first poem,
I see your tears drop one by one
over the stitches, giving her life—
and then, as she once did in the park
when she wheeled you proudly past the other mothers

she whispers with her smoker's rasp,
"The kid *is* cute, you gotta admit."

Betty the Roo

cuddles in her own sling pouch
twig-thin legs outthrust
licks one, then the other
eyes long-lashed, starlet-like

mother hit by a car, joey
tucked tight inside her pouch
at the sanctuary now
suckled by bottle milk

seven months big, big
enough for sun and grass
Kangaroo Dundee takes her
shopping in a cart

traveling north to Urulu
we stop to picnic outside
the store. Inside
the long freezer,

long
kangaroo tails
for sale

What the Barracuda Said to the Snorkelers in Belize

After Charles Simic

Imagination is the screw
that turns you
Longer bait crimps your
short fishing lines
Lionfish bristle with spears against you
but taste like paradise in your mouth
You believe you'll return to aqua waters
Yet when you do, the color always changes
My envelope holds your winning
flower
You, Focker, chug five seconds

You will never grow enough hair with prescription drugs
to cover your bald spot
Your girlfriend will choose the diamond ring
over moving in with you
If you dream a complete house
then expect a mortgage
When you bring five grand to poker
you'll regret those Jack and Sevens
(and when did you last change
your underwear?)
Beer bitch, another "Belikan"

A cab going north only heads
in one direction
The body's chief comfort
Is the delusion of the soul
If you never have children, you will always regret it
If you have children, you will always regret it
My silence is an act—I speak volumes
under water

Write this. Live that
Chug five seconds

Her

When I read the horoscope of the new grandbaby,
quintuple Scorpio, future scientist with steel-jaws,
on *her* I pin all our futures.
"Save up for *her* college," my son makes me promise.
But *she* won't need it, I say.
She is too smart for Need.

The lace baptismal dress—once *her* father's,
my son's—I hand now to *her* mother,
with fine linens Nonna once handed me.
I say, for *her*, when she is bigger.

The last lakeside dinner with the boys
and girlfriends, before they all scatter,
their father and his new wife,
and *she*, queen of the sky,
glue for a Humpty Dumpty family—
love to solid us up again.

Wind blowing laughter gently past us,
as if it knew, white boats sailing in the blue
not going to be. Tiny feet, tiny toes,
tiny white socks: who will *she* become?
marry? what red trike will *she* ride?

Enough of a reason
for *her* parents to marry soon.
The unplanned *she*
in my son's botched Ph.D. plans,
she, so worth it, tiny prize,

a pink ribbon in *her* hair

           braid the poem, *she*

I Am of Two Minds

The one always happy lets me do things I like
The other makes me do things I should

Mind Two may feel guilty over Mind One's frivolity
And Mind One wishes Mind Two would stop dragging her down

Mind One thinks we should stay up late, binge-watching Silicon Valley
Mind Two wants to sleep to be prepared for work

One wears skirts because I have good legs
Two prefers the practicality of pants

One likes romantic films and scary monsters
Two likes Animal Planet and documentaries

Mind Number One: I need another boyfriend, to be truly happy
Mind Number Two: done with men

Mind One wants to buy a fast car *en vogue*
Mind Two plans to buy a Prius

I am planning to erase her like a hard drive when she falls asleep early
(I have half a mind to do this)

Little Red Trucker

In my heart I know you're right
In my heart I think I should never have agreed
In my heart I felt this would end badly
In my heart I bleed for time wasted
In my heart I age by centuries
And turn grey and withered like a wasted peach
In my heart I step out the front door
And float up to the clouds
Where my heart agrees

(My heart, my heart, my little red trucker)

I will end like the children at the beach
Digging in the sand in joy

Elevator

The door opens
I step into a space maybe fifty square feet
a mirror on one side.
Is this the day it will come
crashing to the shaft-floor,
my body splat against ceiling
as we shuttle down?

Or, the door opens
on the next floor and an hombre steps in,
dark and broody,
slams me against the wall,
and, as they say, has his way with me—
slam bam thank you ma'am.

A third option: the door opens
and someone I know enters,
and we sum up the last ten years,
smiles, a wave of the hand,
endorphin triggers.

Or a languid fourth: the door opens
but no one enters. The elevator shifts
obediently to its final destination,
where no one waits.
How long before I see
the doctor? what should I cook
for dinner? Did I pay that bill?

More likely, just a moment of collection,
that miracle of elevation or descent—
to lift, to carry, to carry on,
the day cosmic and complete,
transport as ordinary as breath.

The Leaving-Home Tale

Fairylike I spun for you three gifts,
my sons, engineers
of all hope.

In the dream of home
I mythed away the specter
of geography.

My first gift was journeys clad in my own
adventure, pitched to the stars.
My second was sacred memory,

rimmed in blue, of soccer games, birthday festals,
boat rides on the lake.
My third: hey, I birthed you.

In you I am.
Wherever you go
always

I go, too.

Notes

[1]Cape Rinderhorn is the name of a fantasy house constructed from junk by German artist Thorsten Brinkmann in his 2016 Houston installation.

[2]The word "amazon" means "without one breast." After their husbands were slain in war they had to learn to defend themselves with great bows; this meant cutting off one breast to manage them in battle while riding. These women were likely Sarmatians who lived in the Carpatian mountains in what is now Romania. This particular battle ensued because the Romans betrayed their neighbors after a treaty had been signed; the Amazons joined them in support.

[3]On a stone beneath the castle at Laugarcio, in Trenčín, a city in western Slovakia near the Czech border, these words are inscribed in Latin: "To the victory of emperors, dedicated by 855 soldiers of the Second Legion of the army stationed in Laugaricio. Made to the order of Marcus Valerius Maximianus, legate of the Second Adiutrix legion." This Diana Veteranorum inscription likely identifies the important Roman leader for whom the sarcophagus was designed after he fell.

[4]This tapestry is known as "The Unicorn in Captivity," seventh in the Hunt for the Unicorn Tapestries, 1495-1505, South Netherlandish, Metropolitan Cloisters, New York, commissioned by Anne of Brittany for her marriage to Charles VIII of France.

[5]The answer is "shoe." Anglo-Saxon riddles (which this poem attempts to imitate) generally do not reveal the answer except through image and detail.

[6]The *aubade* is the dawn song conventionally offered to his beloved when the courtly lover must leave without notice (here offered to him by her).

[7]Enchanted Rock is a large pink granite hill located in Fredericksburg, Texas, believed by the local Tonkawa, Apache, and Comanche Indians to command magical and spiritual power. Ghost fires were believed to flicker from its top; at night the Indians heard what geology attributes to nightly contraction after daily sun-heat: a groaning that gave the granite hill its name "Crying Rock."

[8]Dark matter is a still-unidentified matter that comprises much of the universe's mass existing in space. In its cold form it consists of particles interacting weakly; in its hot form, of particles that emerged as a result of the Big Bang. Because it emits no light, it cannot be seen. However, it exerts an influence on other bodies through gravitational pull.

[9]In reference to "Area Code" (1962), a steel, cast iron, and lead work of art constructed by sculptor Jim Love and exhibited by the Alley Theater in Houston, Texas.

[10]These words the Catholic priest utters after the penitent confesses: "I forgive you for your sins."

[11]A reference to the Akan linguist staff from Ghana whose top is crowned by a gold elephant, designed from wood and gold leaf during the 19th-20th centuries. The big-eared elephant, towering above all other animals, like the king of a tribe commands because he can hear and, therefore, understand everything. Accordingly, the linguist who bears the staff interprets and translates what foreign tribesmen say.

Acknowledgments

Some poems in this collection first appeared in the following journals and anthologies, often in slightly different form.

"At the Breton Abbey of St. Gildas de Rhuys," *"Aventure,"* "The Château de Comper," "Migration," "The Night the Books Fell," and "Unicorn," in *New Crops from Old Fields: Eight Medievalist Poets*, ed. Oz Hardwick (York, UK: Stairwell Press, Ltd., 2015), 17-20, 30.

"The Château de Comper," *Houston Poetry Fest 2014 Anthology* (Houston: Houston Poetry Fest, 2014), 26.

"Enchanted Rock," *2016 Texas Poetry Calender* (Albuquerque, NM: Dos Gatos Press, 2015), March 20-26, Vernal Equinox (poem nominated for a 2016 Pushcart Prize); repr. *Poetry at Roundtop 2017 Anthology*; repr. And in the 2018 *Best of Texas Poetry Calendar: Editors' Selections from the Past Nine Years,* April 22-28.

"Cactus Wren," and "Ferroglyph: Jim Love's *Area Code,"* *Weaving the Terrain: 100-Word Southwestern Poems,* ed. David Meischen and Scott Wiggerman (Albuquerque, NM: Dos Gatos Press, 2017) 49, 138.

"Homage to Neptune," *Harbinger Asylum* 6, ed. Dustin Pickering (Transcendent Zero Press, 2017): 24.

"Homecoming," *Red Sky | poetry on the global epidemic of violence against women,* ed. Melissa Hassard, Gabrielle Langley, and Stacy Nigliazzo (Wilmington, N.C: Sable Books, 2016), 95.

"I Go Back to October 1944," *Ilanot Review: "Migration,"* co-ed. Joan Leegant and Katherine Durham Oldmixon 5 (Winter, 2015), https://ilanot.wordpress.com/i-go-back-to-october-1944/

"Litany for Our Lady of Headlines," *Degenerates: Voices for Peace* (Charleston, S.C.: Weasel Press, 2015), 24.

"Migration," *Round Top Festival Institute Presents the Thirteenth Annual Poetry at Roundtop Festival Hill 2014 Anthology* (Round Top, TX: Poetry at Round Top Festival, 2014), 33.

"Spit," *Feminine Rising: Voices for Power and Invisibility,* ed. Andrea Fekete and Lara Lillibridge, forthcoming, Cynren Press.

"Stitches," *Houston Poetry Fest 2015 Anthology* (Houston: Houston Poetry Fest, 2015).

In Appreciation

I am thankful for the various institutions in whose poetry and writing or craft workshops many of these poems first took shape or were revised over the past five years, and to those fellow poets, whether members or leaders, who generously suggested changes that helped: Houston Inprint's various workshops, both short and long; Houston Public Poetry's workshops; the Annual Poetry Festival at Roundtop, Texas; University of Houston's Boldface Conferences; Sarah Lawrence's Writing Institute workshops, including the Joseph Pappaleo Writing and Art Workshop, at Cetara, Italy; Palm Beach Poetry Festival's Annual Conference; *River Styx's* Big River Writers' Conference, St. Louis, MO; and most especially, the Galveston Poetry Roundtable.

I am also grateful to the Modern Language Association of America, the Medieval Academy of America, the New Chaucer Society, and the Medieval Institute at Western Michigan University for their willingness to allow me to organize medievalist poetry sessions and open mic readings at their annual conferences between 2014 and 2016.

In addition, I have so appreciated help and support in what I like to describe as an unofficial traveling low-impact MFA residency provided along the way in nine-week, one week, and afternoon workshops or manuscript readings by poets Lauren Berry, Malachi Black, Hayan Charara, Kathryn Curto, Patricia Dixon, Justine Post, Sasha West, Robin Davidson, Jason Schliemann, Oz Hardwick, Marge Piercy, Kevin Prufer, Kevin Young, Tomas Q. Morin, Gregory Pardlo, Sharon Olds, Ellen Bass, Patricia Smith, Dorianne Laux, Jane Hirshfield, Gregory Orr, Jericho Brown, Eduardo Corral, Sasha West, Justin Post, John Gorman, and Nick Flynn, among others.

Thanks also for the readings and open mics that provided opportunities to write or try out new poems, especially those organized by Robert Clark (Houston Inprint's First Fridays), Mary Wemple's Words and Art, David Cowan's Gulf Coast Poetry Readings, Donna Perkins's Archway Art Gallery Readings, and John Gorman's Hurricane Expulsion and Mardi Gras Readings in Galveston.

Jane Chance is the Andrew W. Mellon Distinguished Professor Emerita in English at Rice University and a recipient of an honorary doctorate of letters from Purdue University. She has published twenty-five books on medieval literature and medievalism and received Guggenheim and NEH Fellowships, among other awards and prizes.

Her first book of poems, *Only Begetter*, was published by Kelsay Books/White Violet Press in 2014. Eight of her poems appeared in *New Crops from Old Fields: Eight Medievalist Poets*, edited by Oz Hardwick, for Stairwell Books, Ltd., in 2015. Elsewhere, her poems can be found in *Antigonish Review, Ariel, Dalhousie Review, Degenerates: Voices for Peace, Icarus* (Trinity College Dublin), *Harbinger Asylum, Ilanot Review, Kansas Quarterly, Lyric, New America, Nimrod, Poet Lore, Primavera, Quartet, Southern Humanities Review, Texas Poetry Calendar* 2016 and 2018 (*Best of Texas Poetry Review*), *Wascana Review,* and other journals and anthologies. She has been nominated for a Pushcart Prize by Dos Gatos Press in 2016 and received an Honorable Mention, one of three, in the Ecphrastic Poetry competition at the Friendwood Public Library in 2017 and in 2018. She has been a featured poet at Houston Inprint's First Friday Reading and at a Gulf Coast Poetry Reading in Clear Lake and a judge for Houston Poetry Fest in 2015 and a Words and Art competition in 2016.

www.ingramcontent.com/pod-product-compliance
Lightning Source LLC
Chambersburg PA
CBHW021154090426
42740CB00008B/1083